ENGLAND WORLD CUP COMPANION

HarperCollins *Children's Books*

First published in Great Britain in 2006 by HarperCollins Children's Books.
HarperCollins Children's Books is a division of HarperCollins Publishers Ltd.

The HarperCollins Children's Books website is www.harpercollinschildrensbooks.co.uk

1 3 5 7 9 10 8 6 4 2

© The Football Association Limited 2006

The FA Crest and The FA England Crest are official trade marks of
The Football Association Limited and are subject of extensive trade mark registrations worldwide.
All facts correct at time of printing, November 2005.
The views expressed in this publication are not necessarily those of The FA or any of its affiliates.
Photography © EMPICS/PA

TheFA.com

ISBN: 0-00-721698-X

Printed and bound in China

CONTENTS

This England World Cup Companion is packed with player profiles of the England team, facts and figures about Germany 2006, the other countries to watch out for and a look at the history of the World Cup since 1930. This guide will make sure you are fully ready to enjoy England's journey in the world's biggest football event.

The biggest football tournament on the planet kicks off on 9 June when the 18th World Cup takes place in Germany. Over the month-long competition between the best football nations, we'll all once again fall in love with the beautiful game and its highs and lows – from the drama of penalty shoot-outs to the ecstasy of a last-minute winner. As football fans, and especially England supporters, we know all about those ups and downs but still we have high hopes for the Three Lions come June. Could we see The England Team lift that famous old trophy on July 9? Come on, England!

The Road to Germany

England qualified as winners of Group 6 ahead of Poland, Austria, Northern Ireland, Wales and Azerbaijan. After a disappointing 2-2 draw against Austria, when England conceded 2 goals in two minutes after leading 2-0, Sven's men took control of the group. Highlights included the 2-0 win against Wales and a classy second-half performance against Northern Ireland in a 4-0 victory.

Sven's England squad will arrive in Germany with the hopes of a nation resting on their shoulders. The 2006 England team is probably the strongest it has been for a generation and even the England coach believes his team's big chance for football glory will be in Germany.

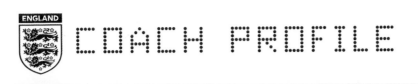

SVEN-GÖRAN ERIKSSON

CLUBS:

Degerfors, Gothenburg, Benfica, Roma, Fiorentina, Sampdoria, Lazio

HONOURS:

Swedish league title 1981, 1982, Uefa Cup 1982; Portuguese league title 1983, 1984, 1991; Uefa Cup Winners' Cup 1999, Italian league title 2000

Swedish Sven became England coach in January 2001 after successfully managing Italian side Lazio to the Italian Serie A league title and Italian Cup in 2000. Under Sven, England have enjoyed a successful period in their history qualifying for the 2002 World Cup. A campaign which included the memorable 5-1 victory over Germany in Munich in September 2001 and, a month later, David Beckham's injury-time free-kick equaliser against Greece.

- Sven's first game in charge was a 3-0 win against Spain at Villa Park on 28 February 2001.

- This first win was followed by another four straight victories and Sven had the most successful start to any England coach.

- During Sven's reign, England have only lost three competitive matches – the quarter-final versus Brazil in the 2002 World Cup, the Euro 2004 defeat against France and 1-0 in the World Cup qualifier against Northern Ireland last September.

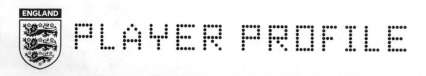

DAVID BECKHAM

CLUB: Real Madrid

BORN: 2 May 1975, in Leytonstone

CAPS: 86

GOALS: 16

ENGLAND DEBUT: 1 September 1996, v Moldova

WORLD CUP APPEARANCES: 1998 – v Romania, v Colombia, v Argentina; 2002 – v Sweden, v Argentina, v Nigeria, v Denmark, v Brazil

WORLD CUP GOALS: 2

As captain and England's most experienced World Cup campaigner, David Beckham will lead his team from the front in Germany. The 30-year-old Real Madrid star scored the match-winning penalty in the memorable victory against Argentina in the 2002 World Cup and, in the 1998 tournament, he show-cased his talent with a trade-mark free-kick against Colombia. Having led his country 49 times since February 2001, David always shows tremendous commitment to the cause – inspiring his team-mates with his tireless running and pinpoint ball delivery. Expect the England hero to continue that determination in Germany.

• During his time at Manchester United, David won the Premiership title six times and the Champions League once before his £25m move to Real Madrid in July 2003.

PAUL ROBINSON

CLUB: Tottenham Hotspur

BORN: 15 October 1979, in Beverley

CAPS: 18

GOALS: none

ENGLAND DEBUT: 12 February 2003, v Australia

WORLD CUP APPEARANCES: none

WORLD CUP GOALS: none

The 2004-05 season was a momentous one for young goal-keeper Paul Robinson as he moved from relegated Leeds United to Spurs for £1.5m in August and established himself as his country's first-choice keeper against Poland in September during the World Cup qualifying campaign. Still only 26, Paul's excellent shot-stopping agility is matched by a mature judgment well beyond his years which has been gained from his Champions League experience with Leeds in 2001-02 and his consistent Premiership form for Spurs.

- Paul has achieved a rare feat for a keeper – he's bagged a goal. He headed in during a League Cup game for Leeds United in September 2003.

- While at Leeds United, Paul Robinson won the 1997 FA Youth Cup.

ASHLEY COLE

CLUB: Arsenal

BORN: 20 December 1980, in Stepney

CAPS: 44

GOALS: None

ENGLAND DEBUT: 28 March 2001, v Albania

WORLD CUP APPEARANCES: 2002 – v Sweden, v Argentina, v Nigeria, v Denmark, v Brazil

WORLD CUP GOALS: none

Still only 25, Ashley made his England debut in March 2001 and has gone on to develop into a world-class left-back. His pacy, attacking instincts coupled with his tigerish defensive abilities has certainly impressed England coach Sven-Goran Eriksson who played Ashley for every minute of England's 2002 World Cup and Euro 2004 campaigns. In fact, his impressive performances in Euro 2004, particularly in shackling Portugal's twinkle-toed winger Ronaldo in the quarter-final, saw Ashley named in the tournament's Euro 2004 All-Star squad.

- Ashley made his England debut after only 19 Premiership appearances for Arsenal.

- Despite his raiding runs into the opposition's half, Ashley has never scored for England.

RIO FERDINAND

CLUB: Manchester United

BORN: 7 November 1978, in Peckham

CAPS: 44

GOALS: 1

ENGLAND DEBUT: 15 November 1997, v Cameroon

WORLD CUP APPEARANCES: 2002 – v Sweden, v Argentina, v Nigeria, v Denmark, v Brazil

WORLD CUP GOALS: 1

Described as the Rolls Royce of defenders, Rio's ability on the ball and graceful pace has made him one of Sven's favoured options at the heart of England's back line. A product of West Ham United's youth set-up – alongside Joe Cole and Frank Lampard – the 27-year-old centre-half has been on the international scene since the age of 19. His only goal for England was the opener against Denmark in the second round match during the 2002 World Cup in Japan. Indeed, his world-class form in that tournament saw fans dedicate their own version of Duran Duran's 1980s hit Rio to the England stopper.

• Rio's transfer from Leeds United to Manchester United for £30m is still a world-record fee for a defender.

• Younger brother Anton is following in Rio's footsteps – he has already won caps playing for England's Under-21 team.

JOHN TERRY

CLUB: Chelsea

BORN: 7 December 1980, in Barking

CAPS: 21

GOALS: None

ENGLAND DEBUT: 3 June 2003, v Serbia & Montenegro

WORLD CUP APPEARANCES: none

WORLD CUP GOALS: none

At the heart of Chelsea's Premiership-winning defence in 2004-05, John has developed into one of England's finest centre-backs. The 25-year-old Chelsea captain has a commanding presence and an ability to anticipate danger well beyond his years, which was illustrated to England fans with a tremendous display alongside Sol Campbell during the red-hot Euro 2004 qualifier against Turkey in Istanbul in October 2003. Useful in the air at set pieces and corners, John has yet to score for England but hit eight goals for the Blues in their league title-winning season.

- Initially starting out in midfield, John has been at Chelsea since he was 14.

- He was voted the PFA's Player of the Year in 2005, the first defender to be awarded the accolade since 1993.

SOL CAMPBELL

CLUB: Arsenal

BORN: 18 September 1974, in Newham

CAPS: 66

GOALS: 1

ENGLAND DEBUT: 18 May 1996, v Hungary
WORLD CUP APPEARANCES: 1998 – v Tunisia, v Romania, v Colombia, v Argentina; 2002 – v Sweden, v Argentina, v Nigeria, v Denmark, v Brazil
WORLD CUP GOALS: 1

At the centre of England's defence, Sol is unflappable, quick and strong in the air. In his nine years playing international football, the 31-year-old Arsenal centre-back has established himself as one of the world's most imposing defensive figures. Sol's commanding presence and influence has seen him captain his national side on three occasions. Twice he has been memorably denied adding to his solitary international goal by officials – in the 1998 World Cup second round match against Argentina and in the Euro 2004 quarter-final against hosts Portugal.

- Sol is the first England player to be named for five consecutive major international tournaments – beginning with Euro 96.

- His only goal was a header against Sweden in the opening match of the 2002 World Cup in Korea/Japan.

PLAYER PROFILE

GARY NEVILLE

CLUB: Manchester United

BORN: 18 February 1975, in Bury

CAPS: 77

GOALS: None

ENGLAND DEBUT: 3 June 1995, v Japan

WORLD CUP APPEARANCES: 1998 – v Romania, v Colombia, v Argentina

WORLD CUP GOALS: none

Injury prevented experienced defender Gary from appearing in the 2002 World Cup with his starting right-back position taken by Danny Mills. It was a big loss as the 31-year-old Manchester United player has a vast amount of major tournament experience playing in Euro 96, 1998 World Cup, Euro 2000 and Euro 2004. His offensive link-up play with former team-mate – and best friend – David Beckham has also been a feature of England's play over the past decade. Gary is one of England's unsung heroes but his defensive skills are not lost on Sven who rarely starts without him.

- Gary has never scored for his country in his 77 caps but he has found the net seven times for Manchester United in 450 appearances.

- Gary and Phil Neville are the first brothers to play for England since Bobby and Jack Charlton in the 1960s.

PLAYER PROFILE

STEVEN GERRARD

CLUB: Liverpool

BORN: 30 May 1980, in Liverpool

CAPS: 39

GOALS: 6

ENGLAND DEBUT: 31 May 2000, v Ukraine

WORLD CUP APPEARANCES: none

WORLD CUP GOALS: none

The 2006 World Cup marks the tournament debut for England's talented midfielder after injury cruelly prevented the Liverpool captain from appearing in the 2002 World Cup in Japan. Steven's range of passing, tireless running and habit of scoring vital goals – for both club and country– make him an invaluable member of England's midfield. Indeed, his important influence is demonstrated by the fact that England were unbeaten in his first 21 matches – during which time he scored his first international goal in the famous 5-1 away win over Germany in qualifying for the last World Cup.

- Steven has captained England once, in a friendly against Sweden in March 2004.

- With Liverpool's 2005 Champions League triumph, Steven was the first English captain to lift the European Cup since 1982!

FRANK LAMPARD

CLUB: Chelsea

BORN: 20 June 1978, in Romford

CAPS: 38

GOALS: 10

ENGLAND DEBUT: 10 October 1999, v Belgium

WORLD CUP APPEARANCES: None

WORLD CUP GOALS: None

Frank has developed into Sven's midfield lynchpin following some polished performances for England, notably in Euro 2004 where his runs from central midfield saw him score three goals in the tournament. In fact, the inspirational Chelsea player scored 7 goals in 13 internationals between June 2004 and March 2005. A feat acknowledged by the fans as he was named England's 2004 Player of the Year.

- Frank was named 2005 Football Writers' Footballer of the Year for his sensational season in Chelsea's Premiership-winning team, scoring 13 League goals.

- It cost the Blues £11m to get Frank from West Ham United in 2001.

JOE COLE

CLUB: Chelsea

BORN: 8 November 1981, in Islington

CAPS: 29

GOALS: 4

ENGLAND DEBUT: 25 May 2001, v Mexico

WORLD CUP APPEARANCES: 2002, v Sweden

WORLD CUP GOALS: none

Joe's eye-catching displays in the World Cup qualifying games against Northern Ireland [including an opening goal] and Azerbaijan has forced the midfield play-maker into the plans of Sven's 2006 World Cup campaign. His international form reflected his outstanding contribution to Chelsea's first title for 50 years, scoring eight Premiership goals, which has seen Joe finally fulfill his promise after years of being earmarked for football greatness. Still only 24, the Londoner shot into the spotlight while at West Ham United with his trickery and ball skills catching the eye before his dream move to Chelsea in August 2003 for £6.6m.

- Joe was a Chelsea fan as a youngster and names Kerry Dixon, Andy Townsend and Vinny Jones as his favourite players.

- Out of his first 19 England appearances, 17 were as substitute. The only full caps were in a 2-2 draw against Cameroon in May 2002 and a goal-scoring appearance against Denmark in November 2003.

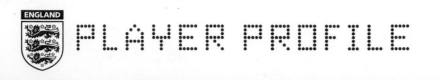

SHAUN WRIGHT-PHILIPS

CLUB: Chelsea

BORN: 25 October 1981, in London

CAPS: 7

GOALS: 1

ENGLAND DEBUT: 18 August 2004, v Ukraine

WORLD CUP APPEARANCES: None

WORLD CUP GOALS: None

Son of former England striker Ian Wright, Shaun burst to national attention with some dazzling strikes for his old club Manchester City in the 2003-04 season. Sven rewarded the pacy winger with his debut in August 2004 where Shaun scored a classy individual goal – that demonstrated his exciting ball skills and running ability. The diminutive midfielder joined Chelsea in July 2005 for £21m alongside fellow England team-mates Frank Lampard, John Terry and Joe Cole.

- As a 16-year-old, Shaun was released by Nottingham Forest who said he was too small to make it as a professional footballer.

- Shaun's dad Ian was capped 33 times for England, scoring 9 goals, but never made it to the World Cup.

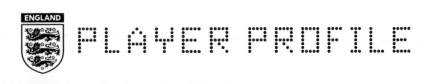

WAYNE ROONEY

CLUB: Manchester United

BORN: 24 October 1985, in Liverpool

CAPS: 28

GOALS: 11

ENGLAND DEBUT: 12 February 2003, v Australia

WORLD CUP APPEARANCES: None

WORLD CUP GOALS: None

In his short international career Wayne Rooney has already become one of the most exciting players in world football. The 20-year-old Manchester United striker had a major impact in Euro 2004 where he hit four goals in four appearances and developed from an exciting prospect to a genuine tournament match winner. Wayne's pace, strength and tenacity is beyond his young years, which coupled with his striking power, makes him an England fans' favourite and the thought of him on the World Cup stage is simply mouth-watering.

• Wayne is England's youngest-ever player at 17 years and 111 days – beating his England team-mate Michael Owen.

• England's No 9 is also the youngest player to score for his country with his strike against Macedonia on 6 September 2003.

CLUB: Newcastle United

BORN: 14 December 1979, in Chester

CAPS: 75

GOALS: 35

ENGLAND DEBUT: 11 February 1998, v Chile

WORLD CUP APPEARANCES: 1998 – v Tunisia, v Romania, v Colombia, v Argentina; 2002 – v Sweden, v Argentina, v Nigeria, v Denmark, v Brazil

WORLD CUP GOALS: 4

As an 18-year-old, Michael Owen achieved hero status during the 1998 World Cup with his brilliant solo effort against Argentina in the second round – a score that still stands today as one of the tournament's all-time greatest goals. From that meteoric rise to football stardom, Michael has developed into one of the world's deadliest strikers and, with time on his side, the 26-year-old is well on course to becoming England's greatest-ever goal-scorer. Despite an up-and-down time at Real Madrid following his move from boyhood club Liverpool, Michael remains Sven's first-choice striker thanks to his skill, pace and accurate finishing.

• Michael has scored two hat-tricks for England, one against Germany in the famous 5-1 victory in 2001 and another against Colombia in 2005.

• The England striker has captained his country on seven occasions in the absence of David Beckham.

DAVID JAMES

CLUB: Manchester City

BORN: 1 August 1970, in Welwyn

CAPS: 33

GOALS: None

ENGLAND DEBUT: 29 March 1997, v Mexico

WORLD CUP APPEARANCES: None

WORLD CUP GOALS: None

After making the No 1 jersey his own following David Seaman's retirement, David James now finds himself the second choice keeper behind Paul Robinson since his disappointing performance against Austria in September 2004 during World Cup qualifying. The Manchester City keeper is a fine, athletic shot-stopper who demonstrated during Euro 2004 that he can handle the big occasion if called upon.

JAMIE CARRAGHER

CLUB: Liverpool

BORN: 28 January 1978, in Liverpool

CAPS: 22

GOALS: None

ENGLAND DEBUT: 28 April 1999, v Hungary

WORLD CUP APPEARANCES: None

WORLD CUP GOALS: None

The pride of the Kop, Liverpool-born Jamie is a whole-hearted defender who was a major reason why the Reds lifted the European Cup in 2005 with a series of sensational performances. It's a mark of England's strength in the centre-back position that Jamie is likely to find a place on the England bench rather than in the starting line-up, but the 27-year-old Scouser is a superb man-marker and tackler who never gives up.

WAYNE BRIDGE

CLUB: Chelsea

BORN: 5 August 1980, in Southampton

CAPS: 21

GOALS: 1

ENGLAND DEBUT: 13 February 2002, v Holland

WORLD CUP APPEARANCES: 2002 - v Nigeria,

v Argentina

WORLD CUP GOALS: None

Wayne is a consistent performer for his national side, attributes that justified his £7m move to Chelsea in July 2003. Injuries and Chelsea's tough competition for places has disrupted the 25-year-old's progress at times but in an England shirt Wayne is a strong competitor both in defence and going forward.

OWEN HARGREAVES

CLUB: Bayern Munich

BORN: 20 January 1981, in Calgary, Canada

CAPS: 29   **GOALS:** None

ENGLAND DEBUT: 15 August 2001, v Holland

WORLD CUP APPEARANCES: 2002 – v Sweden,

v Argentina

WORLD CUP GOALS: None

Owen is a versatile member of the World Cup squad who can play in a number of positions across the midfield as well as at right-back. The Bayern Munich star is a dogged competitor known for his tireless running and fitness. Sven has often shown faith in the 25-year-old player in big tournaments calling on him to add energy to the England side or to disrupt the opposition during games.

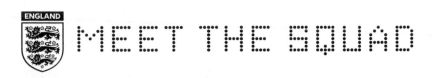

LUKE YOUNG

CLUB: Charlton Athletic

BORN: 19th July 1979 in Harlow

CAPS: 7

GOALS: None

ENGLAND DEBUT: May 2005, v USA

WORLD CUP APPEARANCES: None

WORLD CUP GOALS: None

Luke started his career as a trainee at Tottenham before moving to Charlton in 2001. As well as playing for the senior team in 2005, Luke won 12 caps at U21 level and six with the U18 squad.

JERMAIN DEFOE

CLUB: Tottenham Hotspur

BORN: 7 October 1982, in Beckton

CAPS: 15

GOALS: 1

ENGLAND DEBUT: 31 March 2004, v Sweden

WORLD CUP APPEARANCES: None

WORLD CUP GOALS: None

The 23-year-old goal-scorer scored his first international goal in the vital 2-1 away win over Poland in the World Cup qualifier in September 2004. Jermain's awesome pace and clinical finishing makes him one of the Premiership's top marksmen and he hit 22 goals for Spurs in the 2004-05 season after moving from West Ham United to Tottenham in a £7m move in February 2004.

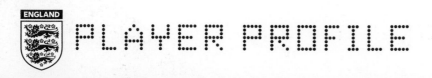

PLAYER PROFILE

DARREN BENT

CLUB: Charlton Athletic

BORN: 6th February 1984 in Cambridge

CAPS: 0

GOALS: None

ENGLAND DEBUT: None

WORLD CUP APPEARANCES: None

WORLD CUP GOALS: None

Darren has represented England at Under-15s, Under-16s, Under-17s and Under-19s levels, and first appeared for the Under-21s in the friendly away to Italy in February 2003. He made his first team debut for Ipswich in the UEFA Cup against Helsingborg in November 2001. Darren was called up to England's senior squad for the friendly against Denmark in August 2005.

PHIL NEVILLE

CLUB: Everton

BORN: 21 January 1977, in Bury

CAPS: 52

GOALS: None

ENGLAND DEBUT: 23 May 1996, v China

WORLD CUP APPEARANCES: None

WORLD CUP GOALS: None

Phil has been a seldom-praised member of the England squad for a decade now. He can play in defence or midfield and although the 29-year-old will acknowledge he is not blessed with tremendous skill, Phil is a robust and dependable player for England. Regardless of his workhouse image, he has been a vital member of Manchester United's recent success collecting six Premiership titles, three FA Cups and a European Cup.

MICHAEL CARRICK

CLUB: Tottenham Hotspur

BORN: 28 July 1981, in Wallsend

CAPS: 4

GOALS: None

ENGLAND DEBUT: 25 May 2001, v Mexico

WORLD CUP APPEARANCES: None

WORLD CUP GOALS: None

A fellow product of West Ham's youth academy alongside Joe Cole and Frank Lampard, Michael is a composed passer of the ball who can also track back to help his defence. After 18 months on the sidelines with injuries, the 24-year-old is now a highly-rated Premiership performer following his move to Spurs in 2004.

PETER CROUCH

CLUB: Liverpool

BORN: 30 January 1981, in Macclesfield

CAPS: 4

GOALS: None

ENGLAND DEBUT: 31 May 2005, v Colombia

WORLD CUP APPEARANCES: None

WORLD CUP GOALS: None

Mistakenly thought of as solely a target man due to his 2.04m-tall frame, Peter is a skillful player with a good first touch and an eye for goal. The £7m Liverpool striker gained his England chance following his impressive 16-goal haul during former club Southampton's doomed relegation season in 2004-05. Peter's stature gives Sven an extra aerial option from the bench should he need it during the World Cup.

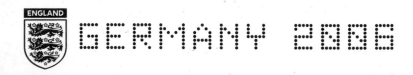

Here's our guide to Germany 2006 – it's going to be a festival of football

A total of 12 stadiums will be used to host the 64 games of the 2006 World Cup in Germany. The opening match will take place in the new 66,000-capacity Stadion München in Munich on 9 June. Eight groups of four will battle it out to reach the last 16 round followed by the quarter-finals and semis.

- The 2006 World Cup final will take place in Berlin's Olympiastadion in front of a capacity 76,000 on 9 July.

- Berlin's Olympic Stadium was originally built for the 1936 Olympics which famously saw US sprinter Jesse Owens win four gold medals. For the 2006 World Cup, it's had a £160m face lift.

- The brand-new £186m stadium in Munich has a very futuristic design. The outside has a translucent, diamond-shaped shell, which acts as a projection surface so the stadium can have a kaleidoscope of colours projected onto it!

- As well as Munich and Berlin – Cologne, Dortmund, Frankfurt, Gelsenkirchen, Hamburg, Hannover, Kaiserslautern, Leipzig, Nuremberg and Stuttgart will also host World Cup matches.

- Look out for Goleo VI the lion and his pal Pille the ball – the official mascots of the 2006 World Cup. Both were created by the Jim Henson Company which is famous for making The Muppets and Sesame Street.

- The whole world will be watching when World Cup fever grips the planet in June! It's estimated that an accumulated TV audience of 32 billion people will tune in to the 64 matches of Germany 2006.

- For the Brazil v Germany 2002 World Cup final, one billion people across the world watched it on TV.

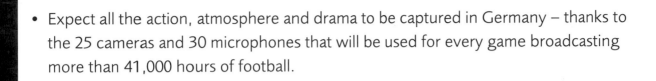

- Expect all the action, atmosphere and drama to be captured in Germany – thanks to the 25 cameras and 30 microphones that will be used for every game broadcasting more than 41,000 hours of football.

- More than 3 million tickets have been sold to football lovers with an expected one million fans arriving in Germany come the big kick-off.

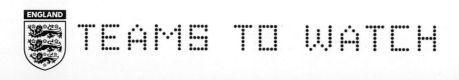

GERMANY

QUALIFICATION:

HOSTS

WORLD CUP VICTORIES:

1954, 1974, 1990

As hosts, Germany automatically qualify for the World Cup and history shows that the tournament hosts have a real advantage. In the 17 World Cups, the host country has won six times and been runners-up twice. As well as having history on their side, the Germans have a formidable World Cup record –winning three times and making a further four final appearances. German teams are renowned for their organisation, determination and big-match mentality.

PLAYERS TO WATCH

Kevin Kuranyi
Caps: 28
Goals: 13

The 24-year-old forward has a fantastic goals-to-appearances ratio since making his debut in March 2003. Born in Rio, Kevin's eye for goal and aerial power will be vital to Germany's World Cup hopes.

Michael Ballack
Caps: 56
Goals: 27

Temperamental at times, Michael Ballack is the creative lynchpin in the German side. The 29-year-old captain was suspended for the 2002 World Cup final against Brazil and will be looking to make amends in his homeland.

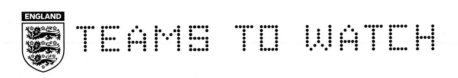

BRAZIL

QUALIFICATION:

South American group

WORLD CUP VICTORIES:

1958, 1962, 1970, 1994, 2002

Despite being the reigning world champions, Brazil had to still qualify for the 2006 World Cup due to a rule change. Qualifying behind South American rivals Argentina, Brazil will arrive in Germany with a heavy expectancy to produce their dazzling offensive football for which they are renowned. Without question Ronaldo, Ronaldinho and co have the ability to win with their mouth-watering "samba" style.

PLAYERS TO WATCH

Adriano
Caps: 21
Goals: 13

Inter Milan star Adriano is a strong, aggressive striker who notched five goals and was named player of the tournament in the Confederations Cup – the World Cup warm-up tournament held in 2005.

Robinho
Caps: 14
Goals: 3

Brazilian football legend Pelé has already stated that Robinho has everything to become better than he was. The 22-year-old may be small in statue but he's a hugely gifted goal-scorer.

TEAMS TO WATCH

ITALY

QUALIFICATION
European Group 5 winners

WORLD CUP VICTORIES
1934, 1938, 1982

PLAYERS TO WATCH

Andrea Pirlo
Caps: 13
Goals: 1

Blessed with fantastic technique, Andrea is the invaluable midfield playmaker for the Azzurri. The 27-year-old AC Milan star is also one of Europe's most gifted strikers of the dead ball from a free-kick.

Francesco Totti
Caps: 45
Goals: 8

He may be a volatile character when things are not going his way, but the Roma star is undoubtedly a tremendously gifted footballer whether as a striker or as a creative link between midfield and the forward line.

ARGENTINA

QUALIFICATION:

South American group winners

WORLD CUP VICTORIES:

1978, 1986

Argentina enjoyed a hugely successful qualification tournament, reaching the 2006 World Cup in June 2005 with a comprehensive 3-1 defeat of Brazil in Buenos Aires. The team's attacking flair is matched by a tough defensive back-line which opponents will find very hard to breach in Germany. This proud nation will be out to better their disastrous first round exit in 2002.

PLAYERS TO WATCH

Juan Pablo Sorin
Caps: 64
Goals: 10

Juan Pablo Sorin is the engine room of Argentina's team, with his tireless running and tackling from left-back. A leader on the pitch who will put his body on the line for his team's cause.

Hernan Crespo
Caps: 51
Goals: 26

Premiership fans need no introduction to Chelsea's Hernan Crespo. The 30-year-old's clinical finishing has been in demand all over Europe and a staggering £68m in transfer fees have been paid for his services.

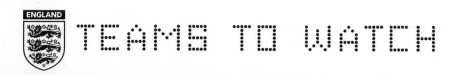

TEAMS TO WATCH

SOUTH KOREA

South Korea's performance in the 2002 World Cup, reaching the semi-finals, was a boost for all other Asian football. Technically gifted with a strong team ethic, the Koreans have now developed big-match know-how.

One to watch: Park Ji-sung

The Manchester United midfielder doesn't shy out of the limelight. A tireless, tough midfield, he is a massive influence for Korea. He's also got plenty to draw on from his experience with United and PSV Eindhoven.

GHANA

The traditionally strong nations of Nigeria, Senegal and Cameroon all failed to qualify for Germany following the emergence of lesser-known African countries including Ghana. 'The Black Stars' could cause an upset or two in their first World Cup finals appearance.

One to watch: Michael Essien

A powerful midfield dynamo, Michael Essien is well-known to English fans after his commanding performances for Chelsea. Could emerge as one of the tournament's stars.

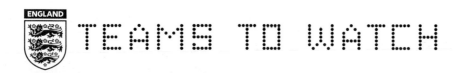

NETHERLANDS

The Dutch qualified alongside the Czechs from Europe's Group 1. With a nice blend of talented youth and experienced major championship performers – the Netherlands could go far in Germany.

One to watch: Arjen Robben
A speedy, tricky winger who has been terrorising Premiership defences for two seasons with Chelsea. Expect the 21-year-old to outpace many a full-back in Germany with his exciting dribbling ability.

CZECH REPUBLIC

After a strong Euro 2004, the impressive Czechs qualified from Europe's Group 1. With a spine of keeper Petr Cech, midfielders Pavel Nedved and Tomas Rosicky and the towering Jan Koller up front – expect big things.

One to watch: Pavel Nedved
The Juventus playmaker oozes class and pulls the strings in the Czech midfield. Even at 33, Pavel is capable of producing a stunning strike from a dead-ball situation or in open play.

Football's world governing body Fifa first held the World Cup in 1930 with 13 nations invited to take part with no qualifying event. Seventeen tournaments on, the Fifa 2006 World Cup in Germany will see 32 nations take part after qualifying from 197 countries that first entered. Here's the history of the World Cup.

URUGUAY 1930

Only 13 teams entered the first-ever World Cup in Uruguay with many national teams not willing to travel all the way to South America. Each country was invited to attend with eight teams from South America, four from Europe and a team from USA. All the games were held in Uruguay's capital city Montevideo.

- World football governing body Fifa selected Uruguay as hosts as they were current Olympic champions and 1930 marked the country's centenary since independence.

- The final saw hosts Uruguay win 4-2 against neighbours Argentina in front of a passionate 100,000 crowd at the Centenario stadium.

- Fifa president Jules Rimet presented the Victorie aux Ailes d'Or trophy to the winners. The 30cm-high statuette, made from 4kg of gold, would more famously be known as the Jules Rimet trophy.

ITALY 1934

The World Cup arrived in Europe with 16 finalists travelling to Italy after a qualifying round reduced the initial 32 entrants. The tournament was dominated by European teams – with Brazil and Argentina sending weakened teams and Uruguay not willing to defend their title with both the very journey and as a response to the European withdrawals from attending the 1930 World Cup seen as their reasons.

- With 16 teams involved, the 1934 tournament was a knock-out tournament from the off. In another change from the first event, eight countries hosted matches – Rome, Naples, Florence, Milan, Turin, Bologna, Genoa and Trieste.

- The hosts Italy fielded a side which included three Argentines of supposed Italian descent who were playing in the Italian league.

- In the final, Italy had to come from a goal down against a talented Czechoslovakia side to win the World Cup 2-1 after extra time.

FRANCE 1938

With the second world war just a year away, the 1938 World Cup saw the shadow of conflict loom large. Spain withdrew as its civil war raged. Austria also withdrew following its invasion by Nazi Germany. Consequently, Germany fielded a side that included four Austrians. A skillful Brazilian team looked impressive until their manager didn't play their two top goal-scorers Leonidas and Tim for the semi-final against Italy saying he was resting them for the final – Brazil lost 2-1!

- Dutch East Indies and Cuba made their first and only appearances in the World Cup.

- In one of the World Cup's greatest games, Brazil needed extra time to beat Poland 6-5 with legendary Brazilian Leonidas – known as "the Black Diamond" – and Poland's Ernst Willimowski scoring four goals each!

- For the first time the hosts failed to win the tournament, as Italy retained the World Cup with a 4-2 over Hungary.

Three Lions lowdown

England did not enter the 1930, 1934 and 1938 World Cups due to a disagreement with Fifa over payments to amateur players. The 1950 World Cup was England's first tournament.

BRAZIL 1950

The qualifying tournament for the 1950 World Cup proved disastrous with qualified teams withdrawing and eliminated nations reinstated. India withdrew because they weren't allowed to play barefoot! Just 13 teams made it to football-mad Brazil, with a mini-league format used in the final round featuring the four winners from the group stages – hosts Brazil, Uruguay, Spain and Sweden.

- To the heartbreak of the huge 174,000 crowd in the Maracana stadium in Rio, Uruguay beat the in-form Brazil 2-1 to top the mini-league and claim their second World Cup victory. Brazil had only needed a draw for victory!

- The Brazilian officials were so disappointed in losing that they forgot to present the trophy, Fifa president Jules Rimet had to go down onto the pitch himself to present the cup.

Three Lions lowdown

Packed with household names such as Stanley Matthews, Tom Finney and Stan Mortensen, England were much-fancied in 1950. After a 2-0 victory over Chile, England suffered a humiliating 1-0 defeat to the part-timers of USA in one of greatest upsets in World Cup history. This was followed by a 1-0 defeat to Spain and England were heading home!

SWITZERLAND 1954

The 1954 tournament was one of the best with goals galore – in 26 matches, 140 goals were scored, an average of 5.38 per game! Sixteen teams travelled to Switzerland with Hungary's "magical Magyars" strongly tipped to win with the likes of Ferenc Puskas and Jozsef Boszik contributing to their four-year, 31-game unbeaten record. All continents were represented with Korea and Egypt the Asian and African qualifiers.

- Austria beat hosts Switzerland 7-5 in the quarter-finals – the highest scoring World Cup match. Another memorable match, for differing reasons, was dubbed the "Battle of Berne" as Hungary beat Brazil 4-2. The game included three sending offs and a mass brawl in the dressing rooms.

- West Germany upset the odds in the final by beating Olympic champions Hungary 3-2 after coming back from 2-0 down to crown a magnificent tournament.

Three Lions lowdown

After their failure in 1950, England fared much better reaching the quarter-finals, losing 4-2 to the talented Uruguayans. The team managed by Walter Winterbottom reached the latter stages after beating hosts Switzerland 2-0 and a 4-4 draw with Belgium.

SWEDEN 1958

A legend was born in Sweden as 17-year-old boy-wonder Pelé inspired a brilliant Brazilian team. He announced his arrival into World Cup folklore with a goal against Wales to become the youngest World Cup goal-scorer. However, French striker Just Fontaine was the top scorer with 13 goals – another World Cup record. The 1958 tournament also saw the start of another new era as it was the first to be televised.

- Hosts Sweden made it to the final but the exciting, skilful Brazilians finally fulfilled their destiny with a 5-2 victory in Stockholm – with Pelé scoring two.

- After their victory, the Brazilian team did laps of honour to the supporters' chant of "samba, samba". Samba football was born and typified Brazil's mesmeric style of fluent football.

Three Lions lowdown

After their tough group games produced three creditable draws against the USSR, eventual winners Brazil and Austria – England narrowly lost 1-0 in a play-off against the USSR for the group's second place.

CHILE 1962

The World Cup returned to South America as Chile hosted the tournament for their one and only time. This World Cup was remembered for its physical play as aggressive tackling and defensive tactics were commonplace – perhaps to combat the flair of favourites, Brazil. After the Swedish goal feast, Chile saw 30 less goals scored and the top scorers notching only 4 goals. Pelé limped off in his second match and missed the rest of the tournament – the World Cup was all the worse for it.

- The nasty nature of the tournament was typified by the notorious "Battle of Santiago" between Italy and Chile. Two Italians were sent off and another had his nose broken by a left-hook from a Chilean player.

- Despite not showcasing their scintillating samba football in Chile, Brazil beat Czechoslovakia 3-1 to join Uruguay and Italy as two-time winners.

Three Lions lowdown

As with Brazil in 1950, England found it hard to adapt to the altitude and heat in Chile. Based in Rancagua, Walter Winterbottom's team finished second in their group beating Argentina 3-1, drawing 0-0 with Bulgaria but falling 2-1 to Hungary. Despite losing to eventual winners Brazil 3-1 in the quarter-finals, the emergence of Bobby Moore and the quality of Jimmy Greaves and Bobby Charlton pointed to great things in the future...

ENGLAND 1966

Football returned to its birthplace as the World Cup was hosted in England. The host country were one of the favourites and had the advantage of playing all their games at Wembley, which had become England's permanent home after January 1966. Brazil were also fancied but after Pelé was again injured falling victim to some aggressive tackling, the champions crashed out in the first round. Surprise team of the tournament, and victors over Brazil, were Portugal inspired by the goal-scoring of Eusebio.

- Before the World Cup began the Jules Rimet trophy was stolen while on display in London. Thanks to a dog by the name of Pickles, it was discovered in a front garden a few days later!

- Underdogs North Korea live in World Cup history for one of the competition's biggest upsets when they beat Italy 1-0 in Middlesbrough. After the final whistle the home crowd invaded the pitch to join in the North Korean celebrations while the Italians returned home from England to be pelted by rotten vegetables at Genoa Airport.

- North Korea also played their part in the 1966 World Cup's match of the tournament after taking a 3-0 lead over Portugal in the quarter-finals, before Eusebio scored four to see the Portuguese win 5-3!

Three Lions lowdown

Under the management of Alf Ramsey, this was to be England's greatest sporting victory as home advantage inspired a talented team to win the World Cup. England had a world-class spine to its team with Gordon Banks in goal, the imperious captain Bobby Moore at the back, Bobby Charlton in midfield and Jimmy Greaves up front. In the group stages, England had looked unimpressive but progressed with a 2-0 win over France, a 2-0 win over Mexico and a 0-0 draw with Uruguay.

For the quarter-finals, the injured Jimmy Greaves was replaced by Geoff Hurst, a change which seemed to inspire the team. After Hurst scored the winner in a nasty match against Argentina, England produced a brilliant performance to beat the in-form Portugal 2-1 in the semi-finals.

England faced West Germany in the final with Geoff Hurst creating World Cup history with a hat-trick as the hosts won 4-2 in extra-time in front of a rapturous Wembley crowd. The match was remembered for the Russian linesman Bakhramov awarding Hurst his second goal in extra-time after it crashed against the underside of the cross-bar – a decision that is still talked about today. The breath-taking final also produced the immortal lines by Kenneth Wolstenholme. As Geoff Hurst smashed in his third goal in the dying seconds, the BBC commentator said: "Some of the crowd are on the pitch. They think it's all over ... it is now!" The Queen presented captain Bobby Moore with the Jules Rimet trophy and England's greatest triumph was complete.

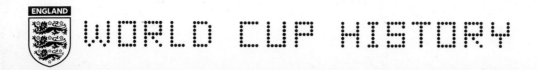

MEXICO 1970

Mexico hosted the World Cup for the first time – it also was the first time substitutes were allowed and yellow and red cards were introduced. The heat was to play a major part in the competition with some games kicking off at noon so they could be screened on TV. Brazil were to light up the world yet again with their footballing genius as Pelé was joined by team-mates Rivelino, Carlos Alberto, and Jairzinho in producing near-perfect performances throughout the tournament.

- It was fitting that Brazil claimed their third world crown to keep the Jules Rimet trophy with a bedazzling 4-1 victory against Italy in the final. Jairzinho scored in the game to become the only player to score in every round – a feat unlikely to be matched.

- In one of the game's lasting images, a tearful Pelé was carried on his team-mates' shoulders after the victory – a fitting finale for the world's best footballer, winning his third winners' medal in his last World Cup match.

ENGLAND

Three Lions lowdown

England were among the favourites to challenge Brazil in 1970 and finished second to them in the group stage, losing 1-0 to the samba stars in a game worthy of the final. It was best remembered for Gordon Banks' unbelievable save from a Pelé header – still regarded as the best save of all time. Agonisingly, the quarter-finals proved England's undoing as leading 2-0 against West Germany, two second half substitutions by England aided the Germans as they came back to win 3-2 in extra-time.

GERMANY 1974

Home advantage proved vital as West Germany led by the "Kaiser" Franz Beckenbauer and the goal scoring of "Der Bomber" Gerd Müller recovered from a shaky start (including losing 1-0 to East Germany!) to reach the final. The 1974 World Cup also saw the birth of the brilliant Netherlands team with their "total football" made famous by Dutch side Ajax. This classy brand of passing football was personified by the trickery and skill of Johan Cruyff.

- The final saw the tournament's two best teams West Germany and the Netherlands meet at the Olympic Stadium in Munich. After a first-minute penalty the Dutch led, only for the Germans to claim a 2-1 win and their second World Cup.

- After Brazil had won the Jules Rimet trophy outright, a new gold statuette was made for the 1974 winners. It was simply known as the Fifa World Cup trophy.

ARGENTINA 1978

Despite protests against the country's political leader – with Dutch ace Johan Cruyff refusing to travel - Argentina hosted the World Cup for the first time. Once again staging the tournament in front of a fervent home crowd, proved decisive as the Argentines with a line-up that included Daniel Passarella, Osvaldo Ardiles and Mario Kempes were inspired. Scotland arrived in high spirits after qualifying ahead of European champions the Czechs, while the Netherlands were again a team to watch.

- Scotland failed in the group stage despite an inspired 3-2 win against the Netherlands with Archie Gemmill's strike living long in the memory of the tartan army. Unfortunately, the Scots had earlier lost to Peru and drawn with Iran!

- The Dutch recovered from their defeat at the hands of the Scots to reach the final. But Argentina, with the tournament's top scorer in Kempes and a passionate Buenos Aires support, won 3-1 in extra time.

ENGLAND

Three Lions lowdown

Following England's golden era in the 1966 and 1970 World Cups, two disappointing qualifying campaigns were to see England fail to reach both the 1974 and 1978 World Cup finals.

WORLD CUP HISTORY

SPAIN 1982

With 24 teams qualifying, the 1982 tournament saw some matches of the highest excitement and quality with the Brazil v Italy, France v West Germany, and Spain v Northern Ireland matches all passing into World Cup folklore. In an open competition, players such as Italy's Paolo Rossi, France's Michel Platini, Brazil's Zico, Falcao and Socrates, Poland's Zbigniew Boniek, West Germany's Karl-Heinz Rummenigge and Argentina's new star Diego Maradona were inspirational.

- The epic semi-final between West Germany and France was the first World Cup game to be decided by penalty shoot-out, which the Germans won 6-5. It was a cruel defeat for the French who had been 3-1 up in extra time.

- Algeria produced a major World Cup upset by beating West Germany 2-1 in Gijon.

- The Italians, who had had just scraped through on goal difference in the first round, won 3-1 in the final against West Germany – joining Brazil as three-time winners.

 **ENGLAND**

Three Lions lowdown

After being very fortunate to qualify – thanks to Romania's shock 2-1 loss at home to Switzerland, England finished top of their group in the first round. Captain Bryan Robson had scored after just 27 seconds – then the quickest World Cup goal in England's opening 3-1 win over the French. However, the second round saw England fail to score in two 0-0 draws against West Germany and hosts Spain and their tournament was over.

MEXICO 1986

Mexico became the first country to host the World Cup twice after replacing original hosts Colombia after the South American country suffered terrible earthquakes in 1983. One player – Maradona, dominated the tournament. If ever one man single-handedly won a World Cup for his country, it was Argentina's diminutive playmaker with a series of mesmeric displays of skills and dribbling which inspired his team and saw him score five goals – one of them the notorious "hand of God" goal.

- The final saw Argentina beat West Germany 3-2 in front of 115,000 fans in the Aztec Stadium. The tournament's best team had won to the delight of the 30 million people celebrating in their homeland with the Player of the Tournament, Maradona, their idol.

- The Mexican wave was born during the 1986 World Cup as fans created wave upon wave during the tournament – it didn't originate in Mexico though, it was in fact a common sight during US college football games.

- France – with captain Michel Platini leading the way – again gained praise for their attacking flair, knocking out Italy and Brazil, before once more falling to West Germany in the semi-final.

ENGLAND

Three Lions lowdown

After a poor start with a 1-0 defeat to Portugal and a dismal scoreless draw against Morocco during which Ray Wilkins became the first England player to be sent off in a World Cup and Bryan Robson left the tournament with injury – things didn't look promising for Bobby Robson's team. But an inspired performance against Poland with Gary Lineker hitting a hat-trick saw the team through. Lineker then bagged a brace against second round opponents Paraguay in a 3-0 victory to see a quarter-final showdown with Maradona's Argentina. The game saw the best and worst of Maradona – he handled a ball over the line to open the scoring later claiming it was "the hand of God" before scoring a sublime solo goal regarded by many as the best World Cup goal ever seen. Despite being 2-0 down, Bobby Robson's men rallied, with Lineker scoring his sixth goal of the tournament – to claim the Golden Boot – and then going agonisingly close in the dying minutes. England were undone by Argentina's flawed footballing genius.

ITALY 1990

Not a classic tournament, the 1990 World Cup nevertheless produced plenty of memorable moments. Hosts Italy progressed to the semi-finals thanks to the sensational form of untested striker Salvatore "Toto" Schillaci who hit a tournament best of six goals. Cameroon, with 38-year-old Roger Milla leading the attack, were the fairy tale story – upsetting Argentina 1-0 in the opening game before finally succumbing to England in the quarter-finals, losing 3-2 in extra time.

- The final was a drab, uninspiring game thanks to West Germany and Argentina's fear of losing and defensive outlook, which typified many of the tournament's games. The Argentines' cynical tactics finally fell apart – having two players sent off – and the Germans converted a penalty to win 1-0.

- Just 115 goals were scored in the 1990 World Cup, a ratio of 2.21 per game, the lowest ever. A total of four matches were decided by penalty shoot-outs – a World Cup record – including both semi-finals.

Three Lions lowdown

Bobby Robson achieved the best performance by an England manager in a foreign World Cup as his team, inspired by the mercurial talents of midfielder Paul Gascoigne, reached the semi-finals. England qualified top of their group and sneaked into the quarter-finals with an extraordinary extra-time, injury-time volley by David Platt. England's next two games were arguably the tournament's best with a thrilling 3-2 win over Cameroon before a classic encounter with West Germany in the semis. Gary Lineker levelled the match 1-1 before end-to-end action saw chances spurned. In a nerve-jangling penalty shoot-out, both Stuart Pearce and Chris Waddle missed their kicks, and Germany were through. Gazza cried, a nation mourned, as the 1990 World Cup was a case of so near and yet so far.

USA 1994

Despite football or soccer not being a major sport in the US, the 1994 tournament was a huge success with more 3.5 million fans attending, the highest for any World Cup. On the pitch, Bulgaria with their talismanic No 8 Hristo Stoichkov had never won a World Cup match before 1994 but ended up in the semi-finals beating Germany and Argentina on the way. Other players to shine included Brazil's Romario, Italy's Roberto Baggio and Netherlands' Dennis Bergkamp.

- Brazil and Italy – the two best teams of the tournament – met in a disappointing goal-less final. It was the first to be decided by penalty shoot-out with Italy's star man Roberto Baggio cruelly missing a kick to give Brazil their fourth World Cup win.

- The final aside, 1994 produced some classic matches including Brazil's 3-2 quarter-final victory over the Netherlands with the Dutch fighting back from 2-0 down. Dennis Bergkamp scored the tournament's best goal with a sublime angled volley.

- The tournament was not without controversy as Diego Maradona was banned after testing positive for drugs while Colombian defender Andres Escobar was later murdered as he was blamed for his country's early exit.

Three Lions lowdown

England failed to qualify for USA 1994 with manager Graham Taylor heavily criticised for his team's failure. Even lowly San Marino had managed to score against England after only 9 seconds!

FRANCE 1998

Thirty-two nations contested the 1998 World Cup with a total of 64 matches played – the largest ever. For the first time in 20 years, the hosts triumphed in their own World Cup as the dynamic French, spearheaded by Zinedine Zidane, proved unstoppable. Surprise teams of the tournament included Nigeria's Super Eagles – who beat Spain in a thrilling 3-2 win – and Croatia who were fired into semi-finals thanks to top goal-scorer Davor Suker.

- France needed the World Cup's first golden goal to beat a stubborn Paraguay in a last 16 game with Laurent Blanc scoring in the 113th minute.

- In a classic final, Brazil, with a lacklustre Ronaldo, had no answer to France in the magnificent Stade de France stadium as "Zizou" scored two first half goals before France ran out 3-0 winners to wild celebrations on the Champs Elysées.

Three Lions lowdown

England survived a shock 2-1 defeat by Romania to qualify from their group thanks to a 2-0 win over Colombia – which included a David Beckham free-kick. Glenn Hoddle's men then faced old rivals Argentina in last 16 tie in an epic match. After an exchange of penalties, 18 year-old Michael Owen scored a solo goal of the tournament before a clever free-kick saw Argentina level – all before half time! More high drama after the break as David Beckham became public enemy No 1 after being sent off while Sol Campbell had a goal disallowed. In the end it was down to the dreaded penalty shoot-out and once again England failed. Another gloriously but ultimately heart-breaking exit.

KOREA/JAPAN 2002

Asia jointly hosted the World Cup for the first time and this growing strength of the game outside of Europe and South America was reflected in a series of upsets and surprises in the early rounds. The opening game saw the champions France lose 1-0 to Senegal, a defeat that the French never recovered from but saw the Lions of Teranga go on in the competition. Euphoria greeted the progress of co-hosts Japan and South Korea. Japan reached the last 16 for the first time in their history while surprise team South Korea claimed the scalps of Spain and Italy to reach the semi-finals. An unlikely quarter-final line-up also included the USA and Turkey who fell in the semi-finals to Brazil.

- Despite the success of the lesser nations it was the traditional powerhouses of Brazil and Germany that met in the final. A workmanlike German side succumbed to the brilliance of Brazilian striker Ronaldo as he bagged a brace to banish the disappointment of four years earlier.

- With their World Cup victory, Brazil had won football's highest prize a record fifth time and had achieved the feat by winning on every continent.

- Champions France failed to qualify from their group – without scoring a goal – the worst performance by the World Cup holders since the Brazilians in 1966.

Three Lions lowdown

England were in "the group of death" in Japan facing Sweden, Nigeria and Argentina in their opening games. The highlight was a tense 1-0 victory over old enemy Argentina with an emotional David Beckham vanquishing the demons of his sending off in 1998 by scoring a crucial penalty. An earlier 1-1 draw against Sweden and a 0-0 draw with Nigeria saw Sven lead his team into the knock-out stages.

Hopes were raised after a comprehensive 3-0 win over Denmark in the last 16 match but the quarter-final against eventual winners Brazil was hugely disappointing, especially as England had taken the lead through a typical Michael Owen goal. Brazil responded brilliantly first through Rivaldo and the with a Ronaldinho free-kick which lobbed over the hapless David Seaman in goal. England failed to comeback despite seeing their opponents down to 10 men and the game petered out to a 2-1 loss.

WORLD CUP STATS

Find all the World Cup facts, figures and records in our quickfire stats section:

MOST WORLD CUPS

5 – Brazil

3 – Germany/ West Germany, Italy

2 – Uruguay, Argentina

1 – England, France

WORLD CUP WINNERS

1930 Uruguay	1974 West Germany
1934 Italy	1978 Argentina
1938 Italy	1982 Italy
1950 Uruguay	1986 Argentina
1954 West Germany	1990 West Germany
1958 Brazil	1994 Brazil
1962 Brazil	1998 France
1966 England	2002 Brazil
1970 Brazil	2006 England?

WORLD CUP TOP SCORERS

1930 Guillermo Stábile (ARG) 8

1934 Oldrich Nejedly (CZE)

      Edmund Conen (GER)

      Angelo Schiavio (ITA) 4

1938 Leónidas (BRA) 8

1950 Ademir (BRA) 9

1954 Sandor Kocsis (HUN) 11

1958 Just Fontaine (FRA) 13

1962 Garrincha (BRA)

      Valentin Ivanov (URS)

      Leonel Sanchez (CHI)

      Florian Albert (HUN)

      Drazan Jerkovic (YUG) 4

1966 Eusébio (POR) 9

1970 Gerd Müller (GER) 10

1974 Grzegorz Lato (POL) 7

1978 Mario Kempes (ARG) 6

1982 Paolo Rossi (ITA) 6

1986 Gary Lineker (ENG) 6

1990 Salvatore Schillaci (ITA) 6

1994 Oleg Salenko (RUS)

      Hristo Stoitchkov (BUL) 6

1998 Davor Suker (CRO) 6

2002 Ronaldo (BRA) 8

WORLD CUP STATS

All-time World Cup top scorer
Gerd Müller (GER) 14

Youngest World Cup goal scorer
Pelé (BRA) aged 17 years, 239
days, v Wales 1958

Oldest World Cup goal scorer
Roger Milla (CAM) aged 42 years
and 39 days, v Russia on 1994

Biggest World Cup victories
1954 Hungary 9 Korea 0
1974 Yugoslavia 9 Zaire 0
1982 Hungary 10 El Salvador 1

Largest World Cup final attendance
174,000 – Maracana Stadium, Rio de
Janeiro (BRA) on 16 July 1950

Most World Cup final appearances
Cafu (BRA) – 1994, 1998, 2002

First World Cup hat-trick
Guillermo Stábile (ARG) v Mexico, 1930

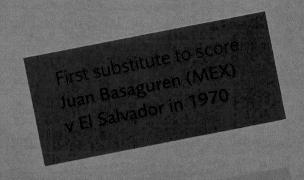

First substitute to score
Juan Basaguren (MEX)
v El Salvador in 1970

Most World Cup
5 – Antonio Carbajal (MEX) 1950-66
Lothar Matthäus (GER) 1982-98

Fastest World Cup goal
11 seconds – Hakan Sukur (TUR)
v South Korea in 2002

Latest World Cup goal
119 minutes – David Platt (ENG)
v Belgium in 1990

Most World Cup matches
25 – Lothar Matthäus (GER)

First World Cup own-goal
Ramon Gonzales (PAR) v
United States in 1930

Fastest hat-trick
Laszlo Kiss (HUN) v El Salvador in 1982,
scoring after 70, 74 and 77 minutes

Fastest goal by a substitute
Ebbe Sand (DEN) v Nigeria in 1998

Most hat-tricks
2 – Sándor Kocsis (HUN) v South Korea in 1954 and v West Germany in 1954 (4 goals).
Just Fontaine (FRA) v Paraguay in 1958 and v West Germany in 1958 (4 goals).
Gerd Müller (GER) v Bulgaria in 1970 and v Peru in 1970.
Gabriel Batistuta (ARG) vs Greece in 1994 and vs Jamaica in 1998.

SIGN UP FOR ENGLAND TODAY

Make sure you support England in the best-possible way - by joining the ONLY Official England Supporters Club.

You get a great Welcome Pack with lots of exclusive merchandise and we keep you in touch with regular newsletters and a members' magazine.

Join now online at www.TheFA.com/membership or call 0845 458 1966 for an application form.

TheFA.com